Writing Contracts
A Distinct Discipline

Writing Contracts
A Distinct Discipline

Peter Siviglia

CAROLINA ACADEMIC PRESS
Durham, North Carolina

ISBN 0-89089-933-9
LCCN 96-83449

Printed in the United States of America

Carolina Academic Press
700 Kent Street
Durham, North Carolina 27701
Telephone (919) 489-7486
Fax (919) 493-5668

for anne

On Travel

With her she would have me go
to Byzantium, the Isles of Greece,
Rome and the Orient,
where treasures from the intellect flow
to cure the spirit
and the mind to grow.

Where once that Poet sought to be,
she would now visit
to indulge in beauty and the magnificent
and bathe her soul in all exquisite.

Yet that journey I need not,
nor (do I think) did He,
for by the chariot of his mind,
in verse He traversed the darkened sea.

By that vessel travel lies
to the edges of creation,
but if more than thought the spirit cries...
nor art nor artifact in foreign lands
my soul bestirs,
for all I need is turn my eyes toward hers.

Contents

Acknowledgments

No book is a work unto its author alone. Thus, I acknowledge and appreciate the contributions of

Victoria L. Cristiano
Anne K. Siviglia
Cathleen Scanlan

Prelude

What laws are to society, contracts are to business. The contract establishes the rules of conduct for a business relationship. Thus, contracts are essential instruments of commerce; and, like any instrument, if the contract is not well crafted, it will produce unwelcome results: dispute and litigation.

The contract, though, is not like any other writing. It is unique. That a lawyer can write an elegant brief is no assurance that the lawyer will write a good contract. In fact, I have seen agreements drafted by fine litigators which, themselves, were invitations to litigation. Here is but one example.

A settlement agreement, providing for the distribution of the proceeds from the sale of real estate, specified that after payment of the expenses of sale and the outstanding principal amount of the loan and accrued interest, the balance of the proceeds from the sale would be distributed according to a formula as follows:

> (a) first to the owner, an amount equal to $27 million less any optional prepayments of the loan made by the owner;
>
> (b) second...

Clear? Yes. Simple? Yes. Correct? No—wrong by millions of dollars. Here is what item (a) should have said:

> (a) first to the owner, *the amount, if any, by which*
>
> (i)   *the difference between* $27 million and any optional prepayments of the loan made by the owner *exceeds*
>
> (ii)   the principal amount of the loan outstanding at the time of the sale;...

The first and incorrect statement of the amount payable did not deduct the principal balance of the loan. Thus, if the prepayments were $10 million and the balance of the loan was $10 million, under the first statement the owner would receive $17 million while under the second and correct statement the owner would receive only $7 million.

To write a contract well, the mind must adjust its focus from other forms of writing to this distinct form; and it is that adjustment with which the balance of this book deals.

Writing Contracts
A Distinct Discipline

Chapter 1

The Contract

§1:1 What is a Contract?

A contract is a set of instructions. It is the plan and specifications for a business relationship. It is the private law of a transaction. Thus, the commercial lawyer—*i.e.*, the lawyer who generally writes the contract—is an architect of relationships; and the homes which these attorneys design are the agreements or private legal relationships within which their clients operate. The commercial attorney, therefore, must *first* think in terms of the various considerations involved in the particular transaction (for example, a non-competition covenant in the acquisition of a business); *then* the attorney must determine how to treat each of these considerations (for example, period and geographical extent of the covenant and those activities which the covenant precludes); and *finally* (and here the attorney assumes the aspect of a builder) the attorney must properly draft the text to embody the decision or result of the negotiation, for if that decision is not transcribed correctly, the consequences can be the same as those that arise from a defect in construction.

Of the three functions—identifying the considerations; determining how to deal with them; drafting the agreement—each is as important as the other. The attorney must attack all three with equal diligence in order to produce a proper result.

§1:2 Form of the Contract

If asked what a contract looks like, most attorneys would probably reply: "Well, it starts with a date and identification of the parties, followed by an introduction or recitals describing the transaction; then come the actual terms of the agreement; and finally, the signatures." For example:

AGREEMENT dated the ____ day of _____ 1995 between ____X____ and ____Y____.

<u>WITNESSETH</u>:

WHEREAS, ____X____ and ____Y____ wish to _____, all on the terms hereinafter set forth;

NOW, THEREFORE, ____X____ and ____Y____ agree as follows.

1. _____
   _____
   _____

2. _____
   _____
   _____

IN WITNESS WHEREOF ____X____ and ____Y____ have executed this Agreement.

_____
X

_____
Y

But contracts, like people, come in many different shapes and sizes—though not with the same variety. For example, many contracts are in the form of a letter:

_____, 1995

XYZ Corporation

_____

_____

Gentlemen:

This letter will confirm our agreement as follows.

1. _____

_____

_____

2. _____

_____

_____

Very truly yours,
ABC Corporation

By:_____

AGREED:
XYZ Corporation

By:_____

Still other contracts, like a promissory note, may begin and end without any formality:

Dated: _____

FOR VALUE RECEIVED, the undersigned, ____M___, promises to pay to the order of ____P____ the sum of $_____ on _____, 199_ together with interest thereon at the rate of ___% *per annum* from the date hereof.

_____
M

And sometimes, as two foods (like beans and rice) are necessary to produce a complete protein, two documents (an offer and acceptance) are required to produce a complete contract:

_____, 1995

_____ B _____

_____

_____

Dear _____ B _____,

I hereby offer to sell you _____ X _____ at a price, C.I.F., of $_____, delivery at your address set forth above during 9:00 a.m.to 5:00 p.m. on a business day within _____ days after the date of this letter, payment 30 days after delivery.

This offer expires on _____, 1995, and it may be accepted only by my receiving your written notice of acceptance on or before that date.

Very truly yours,

_____

S

_____, 1995

_____ S _____

_____

_____

Dear _____ S _____,

I hereby accept the offer in your letter to me of _____, 1995 to sell me _____ X _____ at a price of $_____, delivery and payment as per your letter.

Very truly yours,

_____

B

The actual form of the contract is of little significance. Though an agreement in the form of a letter may appear to the parties less formidable than the formal agreement described at the beginning of this section, the attorney must not be seduced by the form: Equal care is required for the preparation of each.

§1:3 Content of the Contract

There is only one provision I know of that every written contract should contain:

> This agreement may be amended only by an instrument in writing signed by the parties hereto.

Apart from this clause, all terms depend on the particular transaction—hence the importance of the first two functions listed in §1:1: identifying the considerations and determining how to deal with each.

Here might be the perfect time and place to catalogue with examples all of those provisions that can crowd an agreement—from date and parties to basic terms of the sale, lease, loan or other transaction; from representations and warranties to indemnities, covenants and conditions; from default to remedies, period, notices and governing law; and on and on, straight on 'til morning. But that litany would put us both to sleep, and besides, law firms have their own form files, and there are numerous books with check lists, forms and commentary. In fact, a fine book of this kind is Siviglia, *Commercial Agreements: A Lawyer's Guide to Drafting and Negotiating*, West Group, rev'd. ed. 1997 (Supp. 1998 *et seq.*) And to the very point of this essay is the author's warning at §1:4:

> Each agreement illustrates the considerations involved in a particular type of transaction and how, in at least one instance, they were handled. In different situations and depending on the negotiation, the same considera-

tions will have different solutions. Understanding the considerations and determining how to deal with them yield the structure and elements of the relationship among the parties. This process is as important as actually drafting the provisions themselves.

A form, like the pattern from which a tailor makes a suit, is a useful and necessary tool, especially when it is accompanied by commentary about the particular type of transaction and drafting considerations. Yet forms are static instruments, while each transaction is unique, requiring a custom fit. A contract is not a document that can be concocted from a list of ingredients. The lawyer, therefore, like a great chef with a taste for the right combination, must develop the ability to recognize the requirements of each transaction in order to determine what provisions are necessary and how to style them to meet the needs of the deal.

The most important contract that I have written in thirty years of practice (and probably the most important contract that I will ever write) was a one page guarantee that did not use the word "guarantee". In the early 1970's, when the market for oil tankers was high, a client agreed to charter or lease one of these vessels to a subsidiary of an oil company, Coastal States Gas Corporation. The client required a parent company guarantee from Coastal States, but the attorney for Coastal States told me that a guarantee would violate the company's loan agreements. I said I would prepare something that would not have the appearance of a guarantee but would have the same effect. I drafted a letter from Coastal and its subsidiary to our client stating that if a default occurred under the charter, the charter would be assigned to Coastal, with Coastal assuming the obligations under the charter just as if Coastal had been the original charterer. The letter did not contain any representations or warranties and it did not contain many of the protective clauses usually associated with guarantees. Under the circumstance, I concluded that it would

be inadvisable to negotiate for them and that they were not
necessary to achieve the required result. The "guarantee"
merely stated:

> To induce you to enter into the charter party dated
> October 4, 1973 (said charter party as the same may
> hereafter be amended called the "Charter"), with our
> wholly owned subsidiary _____,
> (the "Charterer"), pursuant to which you chartered the
> oil tank vessel _____ to Charterer for
> a period of three years, fifteen days more or less, and in
> consideration thereof, we agree that if Charterer defaults
> in the performance of any of its obligations under the
> Charter, we will, upon receipt of notice of such default
> (i) promptly cause Charterer to remedy such default, or
> (ii) within four (4) days after receipt of such notice,
> cause the Charter to be assigned to us by Charterer so
> that effective as of October 4, 1973, we shall be entitled
> to all the rights and be responsible for all the obligations
> of Charterer under the Charter, as if the Charter had
> originally been made with us as Charterer. If the default
> is not cured within four (4) days after receipt of such
> notice, the Charter shall be deemed, as provided under
> (ii) above, to have been assigned to us.

Subsequently, the tanker market collapsed and Coastal's
subsidiary defaulted, claiming, frivolously, that the change in
market conditions had frustrated the contract, thereby releas-
ing it from its obligations. We immediately commenced an
arbitration proceeding against Coastal, but Coastal, hoping to
find sanctuary in the courts where deep pockets and the
opportunities for delay favor the defendant, countered that it
was not bound by the arbitration clause in the charter. The
court disagreed, and quoting the entire guarantee in its opin-
ion, concluded:

> Nothing could be more clear than that Coastal under-
> took to guarantee performance of all covenants of the
> charter and did so by making itself party to it.

The matter never did go to arbitration. Shortly after this adverse decision, Coastal paid our client several million dollars in settlement.

The foregoing example is positive reinforcement of the principle that the lawyer must create a contract, regardless of its form, that responds to the needs of the transaction. The following example is negative reinforcement of that very principle.

The owner of a significant parcel of real estate in Manhattan gave a potential purchaser the option to buy the property. However, in drafting the option agreement, the attorneys for the owner violated the prime directive governing options: The option must contain the entire contract of sale, leaving no term to be negotiated when the option is exercised. Siviglia, *supra*, §12:1. The following paragraphs from the complaint, tying up the property in litigation, reveal the error:

> Pursuant to the Agreement, if [Plaintiff] exercised the option on or before _____X_____, 1995, then [Plaintiff] and [Defendant] were to enter into a definitive Contract of Sale of the Premises.... The Agreement expressly provided that the Contract of Sale was to be "reasonably satisfactory to [Plaintiff] and its counsel."
>
> Prior to _____X_____, 1995, [Plaintiff] attempted to exercise the option granted to [Plaintiff] under the Agreement and advised defendant that it was ready, willing and able to enter into a contract of sale and make the required deposit.
>
> [Defendant], in response to [Plaintiff's] exercise of its option, proposed a contract of sale that contained terms that were not reasonably satisfactory to [Plaintiff] and its counsel. Among other things, [Defendant's] proposed contract (i) would have required....

Through experience and diligent application to the problem, the lawyer must emulate an eagle, with vision from horizon to horizon—and not a mole, burrowing among clauses with no perspective to judge whether or how they fit a particular transaction or to see other relevant provisions beyond the confines of its tunnel. Recognizing and accepting this mandate are essential for the successful flight of the fledgling commercial attorney.

Chapter 2

Drafting the Contract[*]

§2:1 Introduction

According to my wife, the English teacher, there are two kinds of writing: creative and expository. Plays, poetry, novels and short stories are creative. This book, essays, memoranda and briefs are expository. According to the English teacher's consort, there is a third category: contracts. Contracts do not entertain. They do not convey information or maintain a thesis or try to persuade. Instead, they transcribe the negotiated intent of two or more persons into a set of instructions or specifications—a blueprint for a relationship. A contract demands precision writing, for the consequences of errors in transcription are measured in dollars. And no easy task is the execution of this mandate, for one of the most difficult of all endeavors is to write a sentence that can have but one meaning: that meaning being the one intended by the draftsman. That everyone "knows what was intended" is not enough. With time, recollection fades and alters; and, more to the point, when the dispute arises, the litigators for each side will scrutinize every aspect of the document for an advantage; for a loophole; for a place to hide. Back in the old days, when I was young, I remember reading about a case that hinged on a

---

[*] Some portions of this chapter derive from Siviglia, *Commercial Agreements*, *supra*, §1:2.

prepositional phrase. An employee quit her employment and moved, claiming severance payments. The company, asserting that she was not entitled to the payments because she left voluntarily, contested her claim. The employee's contract provided that she was entitled to the payments "on termination of her employment by the Company". The employee read "by the Company" as modifying "employment"; the company, on the other hand, argued that the phrase modified "termination". Although, grammatically, the employee had the better argument (generally, an adjectival prepositional phrase modifies the noun to which it is closer), the issue is not free from doubt. From the employee's point of view, the text should have read "on termination of her employment with the Company"; from the company's perspective, it should have read "on termination by the Company of her employment". Nitpicking? Perhaps; but someone's money flowed on the turn of the nit.

Now that the stage is set, the obligatory comment must be: An encyclopedia can be written.... But I am old now, so there isn't enough time left. Besides, a lawyer drafting a contract does not have time to consult a reference work on every phrase. In fact, only in special circumstances will an attorney check the law on a point he or she is drafting. If the lawyer went into this level of detail, the contract would never be written. What the lawyer must do, therefore, is examine the document as if someone whom the lawyer hates had written it; as if the finest litigator on the planet were going to review it from an adversary's point of view. The lawyer must become sensitive, not to legalese, but to the English language, to what the words are actually saying rather than what the lawyer intends or expects them to say. The difficulty, of course, is that the writer is inclined to read his or her own words to mean what the writer intends. Thus, the writer must approach the text like one who has not written it, like an English teacher grading essays.

§2:2 The Prime Directive

A contract being a set of instructions, the prime directive must be: State the direction accurately and as simply as possible. I purposely did not say: "State the direction clearly", because a direction can be clear:

- "Excuse me, can you tell me where the ladies' room is?"
- "The ladies' room? Yes. Straight down this hall, first door on your right."

And it can be wrong: The first door on the right is the men's room. Accuracy and simplicity are, therefore, the goals; in combination, they produce clarity.

The prime directive, though, with purpose, reads: "State the direction accurately and *as simply as possible*"—not "accurately and simply". Sometimes the concepts, themselves, are complex, so the transcription cannot always be "simple" in the purest sense. In writing contracts, "simple" is relative; of necessity, it is a function of accuracy, which is paramount. This dependency, though, must not become an excuse for laziness. The lawyer must fight—that is, the lawyer must edit and re-edit—to state even complex terms as simply as possible.

In order not to divert the reader from this exciting, fast-paced dissertation, I have included in an appendix to this chapter (rather than here) an agreement granting an employee what is commonly called "phantom stock". Valuation of this stock is an essential part of the contract, and the valuation formula is an example of why "simple" in the purest sense cannot always be achieved in contract writing. The formula was not the lawyer's concoction. The lawyer's function was to transcribe that formula correctly and as simply as possible, so that when applied step by step, it would produce the intended result.

Later in this work there is also a chapter dealing in greater detail with the topic of simplicity. Now, though, I would like to introduce some friends who can help implement the prime directive.

§2:3 Techniques and Rules to Implement the Prime Directive

1. *Read the text aloud to yourself—especially complicated provisions.* Reading the provisions aloud will often reveal an error that may hide successfully when the text is read silently. Compared to reading silently, reading aloud requires the reader to focus on each word and, therefore, to read more slowly. This more deliberate process allows the mind a better chance to grasp the literal meaning of the words and hopefully to compare that meaning with the message actually intended.

Having another attorney read the contract can also be helpful, but this assistance is not a substitute for the draftsman's responsibility. The draftsman should understand the transaction as well as if not better than anyone else, and so the draftsman generally should be the best qualified to determine whether the language correctly transcribes the client's intent.

2. *Be patient.* Setting the contract aside for a while—preferably overnight—and then rereading it is also a useful device. This period of separation from the text develops an objectivity that reading the words over and over without a break fails to do.

Also, when experiencing difficulty in conceiving or writing a particular provision, it is often helpful to work on another part of the agreement or to stop altogether and turn to something else, rather than trying to force a solution. This separation will allow the mind to work on the problem subconsciously, without pressure, as it does when a person cannot remember a name or a place and, after moving to another subject, recalls the information sometime later.

3. *State the instruction once; avoid repetition.* If repetition is necessary, use the same language in each instance in order to avoid the risk of different interpretations, which are the fabric from which litigators style their suits.

4. *Use recitals or "WHEREAS" clauses that introduce the agreement only to establish background or consideration and to define terms.* This principle is but a variation of rule 3 above. Preambles should never state or summarize terms that follow in the operative part of the contract, lest an ambiguity or inconsistency occur—both grist for the litigator's mill. Recitals should end as the italicized portion of the following example, leaving to the operative portion of the contract the actual terms of the transaction:

> WHEREAS, ____x____ wishes to sell to ____Y____ and ____Y____ wishes to purchase from ____x____ a 1948, four-door, green Studebaker convertible sedan, vehicle registration number _____
> (the "Automobile"), *all on the terms hereinafter set forth*;
> NOW, THEREFORE, the parties hereby agree as follows.

5. *Be careful in placing modifiers, especially prepositional phrases and clauses.* The example of the severance pay dispute at the opening of this chapter attests to one of the most common problems in drafting: placement of the modifier. The writer knows his or her intent and automatically associates the modifier with the term it should modify. The reader, however, does not reside between the writer's ears, so to the reader the result can be quite different—even humorous (or perhaps insulting):

> Dear Bill,
> As you do not wish to exercise your options at this time, I am returning your check and the notice of exercise. I just don't feel real comfortable sitting on a check from anyone of this size.

Another example? Note the literal difference in meaning between the following two sentences, though the writer's intent in the first is clearly the statement made in the second:

> Never include a provision in a contract which you do not understand.

vs.

> Never include in a contract a provision which you do not understand.

Errors in placement are most readily discerned by setting the document aside for a while and then rereading it.

6. *Choose the right words and the right grammatical structure.* The severance example at the opening of this chapter also attests to the importance of choosing the right word. A common provision in contracts is that notice be given by a certain time. Often the clause will read "within thirty days of ____x____ date". This expression can apply to either the thirty days *before* or the thirty days *after* ____x____ date. Depending on the intent, the provision should read "within the thirty days [*prior to/following/before or after*] ____x____ date".

Lawyers are fond of using the words "such" and "said" to avoid repeating long expressions, but if there are two possible antecedents, an ambiguity can result:

> ... will pay $10,000 on *each anniversary* of the delivery and acceptance of the ship under this charter commencing with the *second anniversary* of such delivery and acceptance provided none of the following events of default has occurred prior to *such anniversary*: ...

vs.

> ... will pay $10,000 on *each anniversary* of the delivery and acceptance of the ship under this charter commencing with the *second anniversary* of such delivery and

acceptance provided none of the following events of default has occurred prior to *the date on which the payment is due:...*

Two other words that frequent agreements are "herein" and "hereof": for example, "as provided herein" or "in accordance with the terms hereof". In each of these expressions, the word "herein" or "hereof" can refer to either the entire agreement or the section in which the word appears. Unless the meaning is unambiguously clear from the context, the client is better served by using a few extra words: "as provided in this agreement".

A first cousin to this verbal threat to accuracy is poor choice of sentence structure. Witness the difference in meaning between the following fragments, the latter two expressing the correct meaning:

> ... the fee will not be payable with respect to any renewal or extension of such contract which is concluded after the year 2001.

> *vs.*

> ... the fee will not be payable with respect to any renewal or extension of such contract if the renewal or extension is concluded after the year 2001.

> *OR*

> ... the fee will not be payable with respect to any renewal or extension of such contract which renewal or extension is concluded after the year 2001.

The "anniversary" and the "2001" examples are from contracts I drafted. Not until the second or third reading did I detect the error. Again, reading the document after it has been set aside for a while and reading the provisions aloud will often reveal the problem.

7. *Do not use terms of art.* Terms used to abbreviate broad concepts: "right of first refusal", "after-tax earnings", per share earnings on a "fully diluted" basis, should never be used because these terms comprehend too many variables.

Alone, the term "right of first refusal" is an invitation to a lawsuit. A right of first refusal is an option, and an option *must* specify all the terms of the contract, leaving nothing to further negotiation. The right or option must therefore state (i) the manner and time within which it must be exercised; (ii) the terms that the grantor of the option must specify to the beneficiary so that if the beneficiary exercises the option, the entire contract will be concluded by that exercise, with no additional details to be decided; and (iii) if the beneficiary does not exercise the option, whether the option will again apply if the grantor wishes to offer different terms to another. See generally Siviglia, *Commercial Agreements: A Lawyer's Guide to Drafting and Negotiating*, West Group, rev'd. ed. 1997 (Supp. 1998 *et seq.*) §§12:1 and 12:3.

Often valuations are based on "after-tax earnings" during a specific period, but like "right of first refusal", the term by itself is incomplete. Should tax items that arise outside the relevant period (*e.g.*, loss carry-forwards) be included in or excluded from the determination? Should extraordinary items of income or loss be included or excluded? Should earnings be calculated on a consolidated or unconsolidated basis?

When per share earnings are on a "fully diluted" basis, shares that can be acquired under options or other rights usually comprise part of the base or the denominator; but should that base or denominator include options and other rights that have not yet vested—*i.e.*, options and rights that cannot be exercised as of the time the earnings are determined?

Again (but probably not for the last time), a contract is a set of specifications for a business relationship, much like the specifications for the construction of a building or a bridge. If the specifications are inaccurate or incomplete ... well, that's why we have litigators.

8. *Do not quit early.* Analogous to "terms of art" are state-

ments which, in themselves, are correct but which fail to specify terms required to apply their principles to circumstances
that are likely to occur. Here is a simple example. A company
sold its business and inventory. The buyer agreed to pay for
the inventory as each item of inventory was sold. The contract, therefore, provided:

> Buyer will pay Seller, within ten (10) days after a sale by
> Buyer of any unit of the Inventory, the price for that unit
> as set forth in EXHIBIT B.

But when did a sale occur: on acceptance of an order? on
delivery and acceptance of the product? If the sale occurred
on acceptance of the order, what happened if the customer
refused to accept delivery? The contract resolved these questions by providing in the next sentence:

> A sale of a unit of Inventory will take place on delivery
> and acceptance by a purchaser of that unit.

The buyer of the business would have to replenish inventory
as it was sold. How did the parties determine whether the sale
was of the seller's inventory or the replacement inventory?
The contract answered the question, specifying:

> All sales of products of the kind included in the Invento-
> ry will be deemed to be made *first* from the Inventory
> under this Agreement.

In contrast to the foregoing, the following provisions from
an employee stock option plan are examples of an attorney
quitting too soon and not dealing adequately with the various
considerations:

> (a) *Optionee's Right to Sell Option Shares to the Com-
> pany.* Subject to the provisions of Section 3.04,
> upon written notice from an Optionee the Compa-
> ny shall repurchase at the Formula Price from such
> Optionee any Option Shares then owned by such
> Optionee which such Optionee wishes to sell....

(b) *Computation of Formula Price.* The Formula Price shall be the highest [*sic*] of:

i.   Fully diluted book value per Share; or

ii.   7.5 times the weighted average of fully diluted net earnings (or loss) per Share over the preceding 3 years. In computing this weighted average the most recent year shall have a weighting of 4; the second past year a weighting of 2, and the third year a weighting of 1.

However, no Option may have an exercise price less than the par value per Share at the time of grant.

(c) *Tax Provision.* In computing the Formula Price, net earnings shall be after provision for income taxes, calculated as if the Company and its Subsidiaries filed separate consolidated federal income tax returns with the Company as the common parent.

The "put" to the company—*i.e.*, the requirement that the company, at the option holder's election, repurchase shares acquired under the option (itself an inadvisable provision and unnecessary, for the company unilaterally prepared the plan)—should have been conditioned on the company's having adequate surplus to redeem the stock. Corporations, generally, may only purchase their shares from surplus; and when one option holder actually decided to exercise his option and sell the shares to the company, the company did not have any surplus. What makes the oversight even more biting is that when the plan was prepared and adopted, the company's capital accounts were in deficit. A subsidiary concern that the plan also failed to address was the company's having some surplus but not enough to purchase all shares "put" to the company by two or more option holders.

Other omissions, evident from the discussion of "terms of art", were (1) failure to define "diluted", (2) failure to exclude from the determination of after-tax earnings tax items (such as loss carry-forwards) occurring outside the relevant three-year period, and (3) failure to exclude from the determination of earnings extraordinary items of income or loss which are not in the regular course of the corporation's business. In addition, I doubt that anyone knows what "separate consolidated federal income tax returns" means.

The company, therefore, developed an alternate solution that did not involve the need for surplus, but did require the draftsman to deal properly with those omissions enumerated above. A version of that solution appears in the appendix to this chapter. It was developed with the aid of the company's accountants, as the original plan should have been.

As these examples attest, the draftsman, often with the aid of the client or an expert in a particular field, must explore the various aspects of the transaction in order to identify those elements required to delineate the terms correctly and completely. Unless this effort is made, the contract may fail to deal with situations that might likely arise: gaps that litigators fill with the mortar of their imaginations.

9. *Do not use "et cetera" or its abbreviation "etc.".* This term only creates an issue as to the items to which it relates. If a contract of sale reads: I sell you my house with the chairs, drapes, tables, *etc.*, does *etc.* include the sofa, oriental rugs, free standing lamps, piano, artwork, *etc.*? The draftsman must carefully examine the possibilities with the client and specify each item precisely.

10. *Do not use the words "intend" or "intention" (as "... it is, therefore, the parties' intention that...");* and do not use *examples.* These terms and devices are unreliable braces for poor drafting. Intentions and examples rarely comprehend all possibilities. Like metaphors and allegories, they are often subject to different interpretations; and, of course, there is no one better to find an unexpected and unwanted interpretation

than a good litigator. The draftsman must forsake these faulty supports and expend the time and effort required to state a correct message.

11. *Battle to avoid multiple negatives.* Multiple negatives convert the language into a foreign language requiring translation. For example:

> It will not be inconvenient for the company not to refrain from not pursuing the matter.

Translation?

> It will be convenient for the company to pursue the matter.*

Multiple negatives not only make the message difficult to understand, but, because of this very fact, they increase the risk of error. The lawyer must train the mind to trigger a positive correction when he or she is writing in this negative mode.

12. *Battle to avoid exceptions to exceptions.* Analogous to the use of multiple negatives is creating sentences with exceptions to exceptions:

> The company will not sell __XYZ__ products in the State of New York other than in the Counties of __A__, __B__ and __C__ excluding the Cities of __d__, __e__ and __f__ in those counties.

Restated more exceptionally, the sentence might read:

> The company will not sell __XYZ__ products in the State of New York, but the company may, nevertheless, sell those products in the counties of __A__, __B__ and

---

* Wrong. The correct translation is:

> It will be convenient for the company not to pursue the matter.

A reader identified the error. What better illustration of the point?!

___C___, though not in the cities of ___d___, ___e___ and ___f___ within those counties.

Or, in a more lawyeresque fashion, the revision might read:

The company will not sell _XYZ_ products in the State of New York, *provided, however,* that notwithstanding the foregoing, the company may sell those products in the counties of ___A___, ___B___ and ___C___ but not in the cities of ___d___, ___e___ and ___f___ within those counties.

Contracts are sufficiently difficult to write and to read. The lawyer should not create a puzzle to twist the mind needlessly.

13. *Unwind.* Lawyers often combine in a single sentence two or more parallel ideas that require different treatments. The message is usually stated correctly but awkwardly as in the following example:

Neither you nor I will write any article or other report for publication or give any speech or lecture concerning any of the experiments we conduct unless, in the case of an article or report, we do so jointly and with mutual agreement as to text, publisher and time of publication, or, in the case of a speech or lecture, unless you and I agree on the text, the time and the audience, and credit.

Often, though, it is better to house each idea in its own sentence. The separation will lessen the danger of error by focusing the mind on each concept and on the different treatment required for each. It will definitely provide the reader with a friendlier path to the ideas:

Neither you nor I will write any article or other report for publication concerning any of the experiments we conduct unless we do so jointly and with mutual agreement as to text, publisher and time of publication.
Neither you nor I will give any speech or lecture concerning any of the experiments we conduct unless you

and I agree on the text, the time and the audience, and credit.

Sometimes combining ideas that require different treatment is so easy that the mind, unless it pauses, will fail to detect the trap. For example, a common and important provision in written agreements is:

> This agreement may be amended only by an instrument in writing signed by the parties.

A natural impulse might be to add the concept of cancellation or rescission:

> This agreement may be amended or rescinded only by an instrument in writing signed by the parties.

However, contracts often have termination clauses. Sometimes one or both of the parties have the right to cancel the contract at specified times or on the occurrence or failure to occur of certain events. Even in the absence of such provisions, a party generally has the right to cancel the contract if there is a material default by the other party. Thus, a provision dealing with rescission by written agreement should be treated separately from the provision dealing with amendment. For example, and depending on the content of the agreement:

> Except as otherwise provided in this agreement and without prejudice to the rights of either party on default by the other, this agreement may be rescinded only by an instrument in writing signed by the parties.

Before departing this topic, though, I must add one stunning example which illustrates not only the danger of combining parallel ideas but also the care required to avoid the agreement becoming a playground for litigators. A partnership agreement permitted the partners to engage in activities outside the partnership business. One partner engaged in outside activities, and a second partner sued the first for breach of his obligations, alleging that the activities interfered with the partner's duties to the partnership. The first partner, asserting that his conduct was proper, claimed indemnity from the partnership for his legal fees in defending the lawsuit based on a provision in the partnership agreement substantially as follows:

> The partnership will indemnify each partner for payments and liabilities incurred in the ordinary and proper conduct, or for the preservation of the business and assets of the partnership....

The partner claiming indemnity argued that the word "conduct" was not limited by the prepositional phrase "of the partnership", and that since his conduct was proper, he was entitled to indemnity. The other partner, of course, challenged this construction, maintaining that "of the partnership" modified "conduct". Had the draftsman added a comma after the word "assets", this latter construction clearly would be correct; yet the better solution would have been to write the provision along the following lines:

> The partnership will indemnify each partner for payments and liabilities incurred in the ordinary and proper conduct of the partnership business or incurred for the preservation of the business and assets of the partnership....

Who was right, who was wrong, who prevailed are all irrelevant: The damage was already done.

14. *Do not do indirectly what you can do directly.* Lawyers are fond of shortcuts, but shortcuts can be confusing; and confusion is but another siren beckoning the litigator. I have seen security agreements which state (A) that the collateral secures the borrower's obligations under the security agreement itself, and (B) that those very obligations under the security agreement also constitute additional indebtedness of the borrower under the borrower's promissory note. When I ask the draftsman why he or she adds the obligations under the

security agreement to the note, the usual reply I receive is "That's the way we do it." Speculating on the origins of this bizarre provision, I offer the following Holmesian deduction:

> In the beginning, a lawyer in the firm was asked to pre-pare a security agreement for an undersecured loan. The lawyer was careful and wanted to be sure that the exist-ing collateral also secured the borrower's obligations under the new agreement. However, rather than amend the existing security agreement, the lawyer provided that the obligations under the new agreement would also constitute obligations under the borrower's promissory note, thereby gaining the benefit of the existing collateral already securing that note. The new agreement then became a form copied by other attorneys who did not question the applicability of these special provisions to their particular transactions.

A contract should not be a puzzle and should not require Sherlock Holmes to divine its meaning. In the example cited, each security agreement should provide that it secures (A) the loan, (B) the obligations of the borrower under the security agreement itself, and (C) the obligations of the borrower under the other security agreements. If amendments to exist-ing agreements are necessary to accomplish the result, amend the agreements instead of trying to accomplish the result by some clever device which may not be understood or which may be overlooked because it is too esoteric.

15. *Do not incorporate one or more agreements into another agreement.* Sometimes the primary agreement in a transaction (for example, a loan agreement) will contain a provision incorporating subsidiary documents (security agree-ments) into it: For example:

> All of the Security Documents are incorporated by refer-ence into this Agreement. If there is any inconsistency between any of the Security Documents and this Agree-ment, the provisions of this Agreement will control; but

the Security Documents will be construed, insofar as possible, to avoid any inconsistency.

The provisions dealing with inconsistencies are defenses against poor writing. There should be no inconsistencies; if there are any, they are due to laziness and lack of care on the part of the attorney. More importantly, though, I find no reason for the incorporation of one agreement into another. Perhaps it is just a variation on doing indirectly something that should be done directly: a product of the relentless, mechanical copying of an obscure provision whose original purpose is lost somewhere in time.

On the other hand, incorporating specific provisions from one agreement into another, though burdensome to the reader, is acceptable:

As used in this agreement, the terms ___A___, ___B___, ___C___ and ___D___ as defined in the Loan Agreement will have the same meanings in this Agreement.

However, whenever an attorney uses a shortcut such as this one, the attorney must carefully check the receiving document to determine whether any adjustments are needed to assure a proper fit. Except, perhaps, for the incorporation of defined terms, I prefer to bypass the shortcuts and draft the entire provision to suit the agreement for which it is intended.

16. *Do not include a provision that undermines another provision.* Most instances of this transgression occur in remedy clauses. The offending provision will state that before a party may begin an action, the parties must first try to resolve their differences amicably. Following is a typical example:

If any dispute arises relating to this Agreement or any claim for damages is made as the result of breach of any obligation hereunder..., the parties shall use their best efforts to resolve such disputes through good faith negotiation. Each party shall designate representatives to conduct such good faith negotiations. Any dispute or claim

> for damages, as applicable, not resolved by such negotia-
> tion shall be resolved by arbitration as provided in Sec-
> tion 7.02 of this Agreement. [*sic*]

This particular clause presents two problems: *first*, an argument, albeit weak and bordering on the absurd, can be made
that a party must first prove a breach in court before it can
arbitrate the issue of damages; *second*, and more significantly,
how long must the parties negotiate before one of them can
bring an arbitration proceeding, and what constitutes "good
faith negotiations"?

The provisions requiring good faith negotiation should be
excluded. Parties are always free to negotiate, and when a
problem arises, they usually try to resolve their differences
through discussion before resorting to litigation. If such a
provision cannot be excluded, then the clause should be written along the following lines:

> If any dispute or claim arises relating to this Agreement,
> the parties shall use their best efforts to resolve such dis-
> pute or claim through negotiation, but at any time prior
> to resolution of the dispute or claim, either party may
> submit the matter to arbitration as provided in Section
> 7.02 of this Agreement.

Never give the litigator a platform—no matter how tiny it is.

17. *Do not include in a contract a provision which you do
not understand.* Sound silly? Witness this excerpt on the subject from a letter I received from Stephen E. Jenkins, a trial
lawyer in Wilmington, Delaware:

> ...I have been shocked by the number of times in liti-
> gation that I have asked more senior lawyers—including
> some fairly good lawyers—to explain the meaning of
> some provision in a document they prepared and found
> out they had no idea what it meant. Indeed, I have just
> finished litigating one such case. The litigation did no
> one any good and would not have happened but for
> some sloppy drafting.

Enough said? Well, if not, then consider the response of a client to the answer, "I don't know", coming from the lawyer to whom he or she is paying hundreds of dollars an hour.

§2:4 Summary

Surely there are more rules and techniques to improve drafting skills than those enumerated here, but, at least in my experience, these are the most important. In fact, I hope I have not tried your patience with too many, for it is never a good idea to overload the circuits. In any event, these guidelines are not a catechism to commit to memory. Indeed, I doubt memorizing them would prove helpful. Their function and the function of the examples and even (*horribile lectu*) the appendix are to create awareness of what is involved in writing a contract. Once the lawyer accepts and assimilates into his or her "lawyerness" the basic principle: A contract is the plan for a business relationship, and the prime directive: Be accurate and as simple as possible, the lawyer will develop a sensitivity to the needs of the contract and to the language, a sensitivity that will dissolve the guidelines.... Thus, as we sail into the sunset, and before the dawn of a new chapter, I leave you with this lyrical remembrance of our journey.

Writer's Rhyme

*Word by word
line by line,
I'm gonna make
this writing fine.*

*I'll reread
'til I know
that each sentence
says it so.*

Check the grammar
and the meaning;
be the critic;
do the screening.
Dictionary's
not for show:
Helps me get
those words to flow.

Watch the diet;
hem it in.
Do not fear
to make it thin.

Simple is
a goal to praise:
Let's untie
that wordy phrase.

Every word
let's be sure
follows the last
with meaning pure.

"Won't be easy,"
so 'tis said,
but effort will
put me ahead.

Word by word
line by line,
I'm gonna make
this writing fine,

even though
it takes some time,
I'm gonna make
this writing fine;

I'm gonna make
this writing fine.

Appendix to Chapter 2
Phantom Stock Agreement

Preface. A phantom stock plan gives employees a taste of equity without giving them the bite of a shareholder. The difficult provisions in the agreement that follows are those in Section 4 dealing with the valuation of the "phantom stock". The valuation is based on a multiple of the after-tax earnings of the company. The earnings that determine this value are those for the most recent three-year period at the time the option is exercised, assigning the greatest weight to the earnings for the most recent year, a lesser weight to the second year, and the least weight to the third year prior to exercise of the option. The after-tax earnings are calculated by making certain adjustments and by excluding certain unusual items of income or loss. For purposes of the valuation, the earnings of the company are determined on a consolidated basis with those companies whose income or loss are included in the company's consolidated financial statements.

Also a bit difficult, though not nearly to the same extent as the earnings calculations, are the adjustments to the number of "phantom shares" to which the employee is entitled. These adjustments appear in Section 2 of the agreement.

Agreement

_____, 1995

Mr. _____

_____

_____

Dear Mr. _____,

This letter will confirm the agreement as follows between you and _____, a _____ corporation (the "Corporation").

In consideration of the services you have rendered to

the Corporation, the Corporation hereby grants you
_____ (__) HYPOTHETICAL SHARES on the following terms and conditions.

1. *Status of HYPOTHETICAL SHARES.*

Each HYPOTHETICAL SHARE will not be—and
will not be construed to be—a share of stock in the Corporation; it will not have any voting rights; it will not be
entitled to dividends; it will not confer on you an interest
in the Corporation or any rights as a shareholder of the
Corporation; and it will confer on you only those rights
set forth in this agreement subject to the terms and conditions set forth in this agreement.

2. *Adjustments to Number of HYPOTHETICAL SHARES.*

If prior to the time the "Election" (as hereinafter
defined) is made, the common stock of the Corporation
is split, or there is a reverse split of the common stock of
the Corporation, or a dividend in common stock of the
Corporation is paid on the common stock of the Corporation, *then* the number of HYPOTHETICAL SHARES
allocated to you will be in total that number of HYPO-
THETICAL SHARES equal to the total number of
shares of common stock of the Corporation that you
would have held immediately following such split or
reverse split becoming effective or such dividend being
paid had you been a holder at the time the stockholders
entitled to participate in such split, reverse split or dividend are determined (the "Determination Time") of a
number of shares of common stock of the Corporation
equal to the total number of HYPOTHETICAL
SHARES allocated to you immediately prior to the
Determination Time. If prior to the time the Election is
made there is any other change in the common stock of
the Corporation or if any stock—other than common
stock of the Corporation—is issued on or with respect to
or wholly or partially in exchange for common stock of

the Corporation, *then* the Board of Directors of the Corporation or a committee selected by the Board of Directors of the Corporation shall, in its sole and absolute discretion, determine (i) what, if any, other or additional HYPOTHETICAL SHARES shall be allocated to you, and (ii) whether and to what extent, if any, such change or issuance results in an "Additional Amount" (as hereinafter defined). The determination of the Board of Directors or such committee shall be final, binding and conclusive on all parties in interest and shall not be subject to review by anyone else.

In any event, no additional HYPOTHETICAL SHARES will be allocated to you on account of any shares of common stock of the Corporation (A) issued by the Corporation for a consideration determined by the Board of Directors of the Corporation to be fair value, or (B) acquired under any option or other right issued by the Corporation prior to the date of this agreement, or (C) acquired under any option or other right issued by the Corporation if the Board of Directors of the Corporation determines that the consideration for the option or other right and the consideration for the shares of common stock of the Corporation that may be acquired under the option or other right comprise fair value at the time the option or other right is issued.

3. *Election to Receive Payment on Account of HYPOTHETICAL SHARES.*

At any time during your employment with the Corporation and for a period of five (5) years thereafter, you may elect (the "Election") to have all of your HYPO-THETICAL SHARES valued as hereinafter provided and to receive payment, on the terms hereinafter provided, of the amount, if any, to which you are entitled by reason of such valuation; *provided, however*, you may not make the Election at any time on or prior to the second anniversary of the date of this agreement.

If you do not make the Election by the end of the aforesaid five-year period, then you will be deemed to have made the Election on the last day of that five-year period.

If you die or are adjudicated incompetent, then, notwithstanding the *proviso* in the first paragraph of this Section 3, you will be deemed to have made the Election at the time of your death or the adjudication of incompetency.

If the Corporation merges or consolidates with one or more other corporations and the resulting corporation is not controlled, directly or indirectly, by persons controlling the Corporation immediately prior to such merger or consolidation becoming effective, then, notwithstanding the *proviso* in the first paragraph of this Section 3, you will be deemed to have made the Election at the time such merger or consolidation takes effect.

If more than fifty-percent (50%) of the Corporation's outstanding common stock (excluding any shares that may be acquired under any option or other right) is sold to any person (other than a person that, directly or indirectly, controls or is controlled by or is under common control with the Corporation), then, notwithstanding the *proviso* in the first paragraph of this Section 3, you will be deemed to have made the Election at the time title to such stock is transferred. The term "person" means any corporation, partnership or other entity or any individual.

"Control" means the power to elect a majority of the directors or other governing body of any entity or in any other manner to control or determine the management of that entity.

4. *Determination of Value of HYPOTHETICAL SHARES.*

The value of each HYPOTHETICAL SHARE will be determined by the Corporation in accordance with the following provisions, and the Corporation's auditors will confirm that determination. The confirmation by the Corporation's auditors shall be final, binding and con-

clusive on all parties in interest and shall not be subject
to review by anyone else.

Each HYPOTHETICAL SHARE will have a value
equal to the greater of (I) the sum of (A) the quotient
obtained by dividing (i) the *"Corporation's After-Tax
Value"* by (ii) the *"Corporation's Common Shares"*, *plus*
(B) the *"Additional Amounts"* allocated to each HYPO-
THETICAL SHARE, or (II) the sum of (A) the quotient
obtained by dividing (i) the book value of the common
stock of the Corporation (after deducting any accumulated unpaid dividends on the Corporation's preferred
stock) as of the end of the Corporation's fiscal quarter in
which the Election is made determined in accordance
with generally accepted accounting principles consistently applied, by (ii) the *"Corporation's Common Shares"*,
plus (B) the *"Additional Amounts"* allocated to each
HYPOTHETICAL SHARE.

The *"Corporation's Common Shares"* equals the sum
of (A) the number of outstanding shares of common stock
of the Corporation as of the end of the Corporation's fiscal quarter in which the Election is made (the "Last Quarter"), (B) the number of HYPOTHETICAL SHARES as to
which the Election is made and the number of all other
HYPOTHETICAL SHARES allocated to others as to
which an Election has been made during, or can be made
as of the end of, the Last Quarter, and (C) all shares of
common stock of the Corporation that can be acquired
from the Corporation under options and other rights outstanding as of the end of the Last Quarter.

The *"Corporation's After-Tax Value"* equals the *"Corporation's Value"* after deducting from that *Value* (on the
assumption that all of that *Value* comprises taxable
income) all applicable federal, state and local income,
franchise and similar taxes in the United States in effect
and as they are in effect as of the end of the Last Quarter.

The *"Corporation's Value"* equals the amount by
which (A) the product of seven and one-half (7.5) and
the *"Corporation's Weighted Average Earnings"* exceeds
(B) the sum of the Corporation's accumulated deficit, if

any, as of the end of the Last Quarter and the accumulated unpaid dividends, if any, on the Corporation's preferred stock as of the end of the Last Quarter.

The "*Corporation's Weighted Average Earnings*" equals the quotient obtained by dividing by seven (7) the net of (A) the income or loss of the Corporation for the "First Year", and (B) two (2) times the income or loss of the Corporation for the "Second Year", and (C) four (4) times the income or loss of the Corporation for the "Third Year". The "Third Year" comprises the Corporation's fiscal quarter in which the Election is made and the prior nine months; the "Second Year" comprises the twelve-month period prior to the Third Year; and the "First Year" comprises the twelve-month period prior to the "Second Year".

The income or loss of the Corporation will be determined on a consolidated basis with those entities whose income or loss is included in the Corporation's consolidated financial statements, and it will be determined in accordance with generally accepted accounting principles consistently applied excluding all applicable federal, state and local income, franchise and similar taxes in the United States and (i) treating as expenses and income, respectively, all taxes and tax credits of jurisdictions outside the United States generated by the income or loss for the particular Year, (ii) treating as expenses all dividends accrued, regardless of whether paid, on the Corporation's preferred stock during the particular Year, and (iii) excluding any gain or loss from the sale of any asset during the three-year period under the foregoing paragraph which is part of a sale of all or substantially all of the assets of the Corporation in a single transaction or in a series of transactions completed within a period of twenty-four (24) consecutive months regardless of whether such series begins or ends within such three-year period. If the Board of Directors of the Corporation determines that the sale of any asset will or may comprise part of the sale of all or substantially all of the assets of the Corporation, then, for purposes of the preceding sentence, the sale of that asset will be deemed to be part of the sale of all or substantially all of the assets of the Corporation; and if the sale of all or substantially all of the assets of the Corporation is not completed within a twenty-four month period under the foregoing sentence commencing with the sale of the asset in question, then the Corporation will make appropriate adjustment for any gain or loss from the sale of that asset, which adjustment the Corporation's auditors will confirm; and the Corporation will make any additional payment or appropriate adjustment to any payments under Section 5 below or, as the case may be, you will refund to the Corporation any overpayment made under Section 5 below. The provisions of the following paragraph will, if applicable, apply to any sale with respect to which an adjustment is to be made under the foregoing sentence.

In addition, in the case of any gain or loss from the sale of an asset (other than a sale which is part of a sale of all or substantially all of the assets of the Corporation under the foregoing paragraph and other than a sale of inventory in the ordinary course of the Corporation's regular operations), and in the case of the sale of a royalty interest or other right to income, and in the case of any extraordinary item of income or expense which is not in the ordinary course of the Corporation's regular operations, then, the amount of any such gain, loss, income or expense will be amortized equally, and taken into the determination of the Corporation's income, over a period of 7.5 years forward from the date of the sale or the date of the occurrence of the item of income or expense, as the case may be.

"*Additional Amounts*" shall be determined as follows: if the Corporation pays, issues or distributes cash or property—other than common stock of the Corporation—on or with respect to the common stock of the Corporation, *then* the amount of the cash and the value of the property so paid, issued or distributed on or with respect to each share of the Corporation's common stock shall—except to the extent otherwise determined under

Section 2 above—constitute an "Additional Amount" attributable to each HYPOTHETICAL SHARE allocated to you at the time the stockholders entitled to receive such cash or property are determined. For purposes of the preceding sentence, the value of property shall be determined as of the time the Election is made. Such value shall be determined by the Board of Directors of the Corporation or by a committee selected by the Board of Directors of the Corporation, and such determination shall be made in the sole and absolute discretion of the Board or such committee, as the case may be, shall be final, binding and conclusive on all parties in interest, and shall not be subject to review by anyone else.

5. Amount of Payment and Payment.

The Corporation will pay you that amount (the "Amount"), if any, by which (A) the product of the value of each HYPOTHETICAL SHARE and the number of HYPOTHETICAL SHARES allocated to you exceeds (B) _____ dollars ($_____).

Subject to the provisions of the following paragraph, the Corporation will pay you the Amount within ninety (90) days after the Corporation's auditors confirm the Value of each HYPOTHETICAL SHARE.

If the Election is not made by reason of merger or consolidation or a sale of more than fifty percent (50%) of the Corporation's common stock, the Board of Directors of the Corporation may, in its sole discretion, defer payment of up to seventy-five percent (75%) of the Amount for a period which will not extend beyond the third anniversary of the date on which the ninety-day period under the foregoing paragraph expires, provided, however, that the Corporation will pay at least one-third of the portion deferred on or before each anniversary of that date (an "Anniversary Date"). If the Board of Directors elects to defer payment under the preceding sentence, it may from time to time thereafter—but always subject to the minimum payment requirements of the preceding sentence—modify any payment schedule it specifies and determine when any deferred payment is to be made and the amount thereof. If the Board of Directors elects to defer payment of a portion of the Amount, the Corporation will pay interest at the rate of _____ percent (___%) *per annum* on the outstanding balance of the portion deferred, accrued interest to be paid with each payment of the portion deferred but, in any event, on each Anniversary Date. If the Corporation fails to make payment in accordance with the foregoing provisions, the unpaid balance of the Amount, together with accrued interest thereon, will become and be due and payable on demand by you.

6. You may not transfer or assign any of your rights or benefits under this agreement or with respect to any HYPOTHETICAL SHARES, and any such transfer or assignment or attempt thereat shall be null and void. Subject to the foregoing, your legal representatives and the legal representatives of your estate will be entitled to payment of the Amount under and pursuant to this agreement.

7. This agreement will have no bearing on your right to employment with the Corporation. Except as may be expressly provided in a written employment agreement between the you and the Corporation, employment is for as long as you and the Corporation wish it to last. You may resign your employment at any time. Likewise the Corporation may dismiss you at any time.

8. This agreement may be amended only by an instrument in writing signed by you and the Corporation.

9. This agreement will be governed by the law of the State of _____.

                                        Very truly yours,
                    [————THE CORPORATION————]

                    By:_____
                        Name:

Title:

AGREED:

_____

Chapter 3

Building Agreements—Outlines and Term Sheets

As stated at the opening of Chapter 1, two of the three essential functions that the commercial lawyer performs are (A) to identify the considerations involved in the transaction, and (B) to determine how to deal with those considerations. Often the client negotiates the basic business terms before introducing the matter to the attorney:—for example, in the case of an employment arrangement: compensation and period of employment; in the case of a loan: amount of the loan and drawdown schedule, interest rate, payment terms and collateral; in the case of a license: property subject to the license, territory of use, terms of exclusivity, period, royalty rate and, perhaps, minimum royalties. Many times, though, the client's information on these matters is incomplete and requires further refinement. On other occasions, the client, about to consider an unfamiliar transaction, may come to the attorney for advice on what points he or she should discuss with the other party.

In these circumstances, experience is the attorney's best asset. Checklists are helpful, and even seasoned attorneys will use them; but since all transactions differ, the checklist must not be relied upon to comprehend every aspect of the deal. As the British officer who led the demolition squad in *Bridge on the River Kwai* said: "There's always the unexpected." In addition, checklists are little more than key words; and behind every door there is an empty room to furnish.

After initially exploring the transaction with the client, I do not draft the agreements. Instead, I will prepare an outline detailing the various aspects of the transaction and its essential terms, which I then review with the client. This initial abstract or snapshot serves two purposes: *first*, it allows both client and attorney to visualize the entire transaction and focus on the essential terms; *second*, by doing so, it allows them to purge any misunderstanding, which so often and so easily occurs in conversation.

From the outline, as revised by discussions with the client, I will next prepare a term sheet for the other party and its attorney. The term sheet is generally similar to the outline. It simplifies and facilitates the negotiation by placing the format and the essential terms of the transaction before the parties and their attorneys in a readily accessible manner. The participants do not have to wend their ways through a forest of words to locate and focus on what is important. The negotiations then produce a final term sheet (not a letter of intent) from which the attorneys will draft the agreements. A letter of intent is an instrument which details the essential terms of a transaction and which the parties sign before they prepare the formal contracts. The letter is not intended to create legal obligations. For the form of letter of intent which I recommend, see the first appendix to this chapter.

I have learned that this procedure of using an outline and a term sheet is faster and more efficient, less combative, and less costly to the client than first preparing drafts of the agreements for the client to review, then revising those drafts after vetting them with the client, and finally submitting an army of documents to the other side from which the negotiations will proceed, producing still more and more drafts of the same documents.

As an example of this approach, the second appendix to this chapter contains the outline for the acquisition of a business in New York. The acquisition involved the purchase of the seller's inventory and its customer and supplier lists. The seller retained its accounts receivable and other assets. The outline not only details the terms of the transaction, it also highlights various compliance requirements and tax considerations. In addition, the outline serves to focus the client's attention on issues that were not discussed. Some of these are easily recognized (items 11 and 16.D). Others are marked by italicized passages in brackets.

After reviewing the outline with our client, we prepared the term sheet for seller and its attorney, omitting items 9, 11, 16, 18 and 19. We reached agreement on the basic terms in a single telephone conversation without any meetings, which are always costly to the client.

Outlines and term sheets are useful in almost any transaction: employment arrangements; shareholder arrangements; partnerships and joint ventures; acquisitions; financings; licenses; distributorships; leasing arrangements; and others that I do not have time to enumerate because it's now time for lunch. Even if the attorney for the other party prepares the term sheet, it is worthwhile to have an outline from which to work with your client. It minimizes the risk of oversight and results in a more efficient review of the term sheet prepared by the other attorney. This will save time and, therefore, money for the client.

Appendix 1 to Chapter 3

"Following is the only form of letter of intent I ever use.

"That's right. I never use a letter of intent. Even though they contain provisions loudly and carefully declaring that they are not agreements and that they create no obligations, they are invitations to litigation. As I write this passage, I am in the midst of that very situation. The letter of intent was signed before the client came to our firm."[1]

---

1. Siviglia, *Commercial Agreements, supra,* §11:1.

Appendix 2 to Chapter 3

Outline of Transaction

**Note: This outline is for internal use only.
It should not be sent to the seller.**

1. *Description of Transaction.* Purchase of the business and inventory of _____[Seller]_____ by _____[Buyer]_____. The business of Seller is the purchase and sale of the kinds of goods listed in *Exhibit A.*

2. *Format.* The signing of the contract and the consummation of the sale will take place simultaneously: *i.e.*, at the same time the contract is signed the initial installment of the purchase price will be paid and the assets will be transferred to Buyer. See item 15 below.

3. *Seller.*_____, a New York corporation

    _____

    _____

    Tel: _____
    Fax: _____

4. *Buyer.* _____, a New York corporation

    _____

    Tel: _____
    Fax: _____

5. *Assets to be Purchased.* The business, inventory, and supplier and customer lists of Seller. The supplier and the customer lists will include names, addresses, telephone and fax numbers, persons to contact, and, in the case of customers, the types and volumes of products purchased during the last year. The supplier lists will include types and volumes of products supplied during the last year and the supplier's standard terms.

Prior to closing, Seller will furnish Buyer with the foregoing information other than names, addresses, telephone and fax numbers and persons to contact. This latter information will be completed at the closing.

Seller will retain sufficient inventory to fill orders outstanding at the time of closing.

6. *Delivery of Inventory.* Buyer will take delivery of the inventory at the time of closing and begin removing inventory from Seller's premises immediately following the closing. Removal will be completed within 1 week. All inventory remaining on Seller's premises will be clearly marked as being owned by the Buyer with Seller having no interest therein. There will be no charge to Buyer for the inventory remaining on Seller's premises pending removal.

7. *Price.* $_____ plus the price of the inventory as determined by Seller and Buyer on the day of or the day prior to the closing based on [*prices of Seller's suppliers current at that time/prices per latest invoices from Seller's suppliers for those items*].

8. *Payment.* $_____ at closing by bank check or certified check with the balance payable in 12 monthly installments commencing one month after closing with interest at the rate of ____% *per annum.* Each of the first 11 installments will be $\frac{1}{18}$ of that balance plus accrued interest. The final installment will be the remaining balance plus accrued interest. See item 15 below.

9. *Security for Deferred Portion of Purchase Price.* [*Inventory purchased and receivables therefrom/all of Buyer's accounts receivable/guarantees by Buyer's shareholders*] See Item 16.C below.

10. *Basic Warranties.*

A. *Buyer and Seller.* Usual corporate warranties: existence and good standing; power to enter into transaction; due authorization and execution; binding effect and enforceability of agreement; no violation of other agreements or corporate documents.

B.   *Seller and Seller's Shareholders.*

    1.   *As to inventory*: sole ownership; no liens, encumbrances or other rights; no litigation or claims pending or threatened; good condition (the warranty with respect to condition to remain in effect for a limited period of time).

    2.   *Customer and Supplier lists*: complete; accurate; no omissions. Seller has not made and will not make any other sale or disposition of these lists or of any of the information contained therein.

    3.   *Sales*: Seller's sales to the customers listed on the customer list were $_____ for calendar year 199_; $_____ for calendar year 199_; and $_____ from January 1 of this year through _____ 31.

    4.   *Taxes*: Seller has paid all taxes owed by it.

11.   *Security, if any, for Seller's warranties.* If the shareholders of Seller join in the warranties, additional security is probably not necessary. Otherwise, a right of set off against the deferred portion of the purchase price is one possibility, but this right is available for only one year.

12.   *Non-compete.* For two years following the closing, Seller and it shareholders will not, directly or indirectly, work for, assist, or invest in or provide financing or credit to any individual, corporation, partnership or other entity engaging in competitive activities in _____[geographical area]_____. Buyer will have the right to injunctive relief.

13.   *Further Assistance.* For a period of three months following the closing, Seller and its shareholders will, without charge, assist Buyer in transferring the business to Buyer and securing the customers and suppliers for the Buyer.

This assistance will include, but not be limited to, introductions and attending meetings with the Buyer and customers and suppliers.

14. *Name Change.* Within 30 days after the closing, Seller will change its name to "_____". Seller and its shareholders will not use any name similiar to ____[Seller's name]_____.

15. *Compliance.*

A.   Bulk Sales Law under Uniform Commercial Code with notices to creditors (including federal and state tax authorities).

B.   Bulk Transfer provisions of §1141(c) of N.Y.S. Tax Law and Technical Services Bureau Guidelines for Bulk Sales Transactions.

NOTE: Simultaneous closing (item 2 above) means that notices to creditors and to the Tax Commission will be sent prior to signing the contract of sale. Provision may have to be made to escrow payments of the purchase price (item 8 above) depending on notice from the Tax Commission.

16. *Inquiries.*

A.   Uniform Commercial Code and lien searches.

B.   Verify that no portion of the sale is subject to the sales tax.

C.   Compliance with Buyer's financing requirements.

D.   Are there any contracts of Seller that Buyer might want assigned to it?

E.   Check Seller's financial statements.

17. *Certificates of resolutions, incumbency and corporate documents for Buyer and Seller.*

A.   *Buyer:* approval by its directors.

B.   *Seller:* approval by its shareholders and directors.[2]

_____

2. Generally, a sale by a corporation of all or substantially all of its assets requires shareholder approval.

18. *Insurance.* Arrange property and liability coverage for inventory and medical coverage for any new employees of Buyer.
19. *Income Tax Considerations.* Allocation of purchase price among assets purchased and non-compete provision; other. [Buyer's accountants to advise]

EXHIBIT A
[List of Goods]

Chapter 4

There Is No Shame in Drafting a Fair Agreement

Too often lawyers—or, perhaps, just too many lawyers—believe that when they draft an agreement, they must prepare the document to reflect only the interests of their client. They pay little, if any, attention to the legitimate concerns of the other party.

I recently represented a client in the severance arrangements with his employer. The agreement, drafted by the employer's attorney, contained, as expected, a release by our client in favor of the employer; it did not contain a release in favor of our client. The agreement required our client to reimburse the employer for legal and other costs incurred by the employer in enforcing the agreement; it did not contain a provision absolving our client from this obligation if he prevailed in the litigation; nor did it contain comparable reimbursement provisions in favor of our client. Finally, the agreement gave the employer unilateral discretion to make certain determinations that could sever rights of our client to payment.

Highhanded drafting such as this is not only offensive, antagonizing the other party and his or her lawyer, but it needlessly prolongs the negotiating and drafting process, thereby adding to the legal costs of both parties and to the mounting deficit in respect that clients and the general public have for lawyers.

In our comments to the employer's draft of the severance agreement, we added a release in favor of our client, we limited the discretion of the employer, we absolved our client from the obligation to reimburse the employer for the costs of enforcement if our client prevailed, and we added comparable reimbursement provisions in favor of our client. The results of these comments were mutual releases, limited discretion, and deletion of all provisions regarding costs of enforcement. These changes were made by the employer's attorney based on our counterproposals without any negotiation.

On another occasion, I received a draft of an agreement providing for the redemption by our client, on the East Coast, of the stock of a former employee located on the West Coast. In the most polite terms, the relationship between our client and the employee was strained, contentious and devoid of trust. Yet, despite this atmosphere of distrust, not only did the attorney for the employee produce an agreement without the mandatory warranties that the employee's stock was free from any encumbrance, option or other right or claim, but the agreement failed to provide adequate assurances that on payment of the purchase price, the stock certificates, duly endorsed, would be delivered to our client. On this latter point, all that was needed was a provision for the employee's attorney to confirm (i) that the attorney had in its custody the duly endorsed stock certificates, and (ii) that the attorney would forward the certificates to our client on receipt of the purchase price in the attorney's escrow account.

The corollary to these observations, of course, is that consideration of the other party's legitimate concerns is also essential when commenting on the initial draft prepared by the other party. For example, in a financing that involved an assignment of charter hire to be deposited in a blocked account pending application to payments of principal and interest as they became due, the lender did not provide for interest while the funds remained on deposit. We drafted a clause providing for interest, which also took into account the lender's point of view. Following is the text of that clause:

> The Assignee will retain the funds that it holds in an interest-bearing account. The interest will constitute additional security for the Shipowner's Obligations, and while an Event of Default does not exist, the Assignee will, on each Repayment Date, pay the interest to the Shipowner to the extent it is not required for the payment [of principal and interest] due on the Repayment Date.

The lender accepted this text verbatim, thereby avoiding one or two steps in the drafting process, saving the client double legal fees for the time saved (since the borrower always pays the lender's legal fees), and creating a good rapport between the lender and the client.

―――――――

I do not know whether it is arrogance, indolence, naiveté, some other factor, or a combination of factors that compels an attorney to produce an agreement that assumes the attorney's client is the only party with a legitimate interest in the terms. Perhaps the compulsion arises from some recidivistic eruption of the medulla oblongata convincing the attorney that he or she will create leverage in the negotiation by tilting the document excessively to favor the client. Perhaps it is the result of our adversarial training and the adversarial nature of the practice—at least insofar as litigation is concerned.

Agreements, though—all "agree"ments by definition—involve two or more parties trying to reach a common goal. True, there is an adversarial aspect to the process of reaching agreement; but unlike litigation, there is also an element of commonality. In some cases this community of interest is more, such as an employment agreement or partnership agreement; in some cases it is less, such as a severance agreement or the sale of a business. But in all cases it exists. Thus, an appreciation of and an effort to honor the legitimate concerns of the other party in the drafting process is essential—at least from this practitioner's point of view—to the efficient consummation of a transaction and the proper representation of one's client. In over thirty years of practice, I have yet to see one side either sustain an advantage by overreaching or "slip" anything by the other side. Invariably, the other party and its attorney—assuming relatively equal bargaining positions—will force the terms back to within the realm of reasonableness. The attorney, therefore, does not compromise the client's interest by preparing a fair agreement; in fact, by doing so, the attorney furthers that interest.

Chapter 5

Themes and Variations—
Additional Suggestions

§5:1 It Is Not Treacherous to Help
the Other Guy

As observed at the end of the last chapter, commercial transactions are not adversarial proceedings. The goal is not to win; the goal is to do a deal that conforms to the intent of the parties. Thus, while the attorney must at all times represent the interests of the client, the attorney must not seek to gain an advantage contrary to the terms of the deal from a mistake by the other lawyer. An obvious example—and surely one that begs correction—is the inadvertent omission of a word: "The Company will pay the following expenses..." vs. "The Company will *not* pay the following expenses...". Do unto the other lawyer as you would have that lawyer do unto you.

In the context of a commercial transaction, I doubt there is a better application of the Golden Rule than to the principle: correct drafting errors of the other attorney. In fact, because the object of a contract is to reflect accurately the intent of all parties, I view this principle as an ethical obligation. Allowing errors that one detects to remain uncorrected serves but two demons: a perverse desire to gain an improper advantage; litigation that should never be spawned. The client is ill represented by this type of practice.

§5:2 Be Aware of Your Limitations

The best philosopher of the Twentieth Century? Why Dirty Harry, of course: "A man's got to know his limitations." I was recently asked by an inventor to review the work of the firm that was representing him in the acquisition from his former employer of patent applications for products that the inventor developed. The proposal by the former employer contained critical language restricting the inventor's right to develop certain products. The language was patent terminology, the meaning and implications of which neither I nor the other law firm understood. I, therefore, asked the inventor's patent counsel to review the language, and they suggested an important revision, permitting the client the flexibility he needed.

Recognition and acceptance of the limits of one's expertise is essential to represent the client properly, and if the required expertise does not reside within one's firm, the lawyer must obtain that expertise elsewhere. If the attorneys who had drafted the stock option plan discussed in §2:3 of Chapter 2 had consulted with the company's accountants, they might have corrected some of the errors. As mentioned in that section, we developed the substitute arrangement with the aid of the accountants.

§5:3 Do Not Wither within Your Area of Expertise

The reverse of knowing your limitations and finding assistance is knowing your strengths and using them. Often an experienced commercial attorney will have better perspective on a matter than his or her client or even a specialist. In these situations, the attorney should assume responsibility and the attorney's judgement should usually control. Two examples follow.

As lead counsel for the development of a luxury condominium in Manhattan in the early 1980s, we retained special counsel to prepare the offering plan because our firm had no capability in this area. Their draft of the plan provided that interest earned during construction on deposits by the buyers would be credited against the purchase prices. I insisted that the provision be changed to pay the developer this interest without a credit to the buyers as long as the developer delivered the apartments in accordance with the sales contracts. Special counsel resisted, arguing that the attorney general would never approve a plan containing such a requirement. I countered that the attorney general would approve the plan as long as the interest arrangements were properly disclosed. "If the attorney general rejects the plan," I continued, "we will be in no worse a position." The minor delay and expense involved were well worth the potential reward.

The plan was submitted in accordance with my suggestion, and the attorney general approved it. At that time interest rates in the United States were the highest in recent history, so our departure from the norm meant substantial additional profit to the client. In fact, another developer, who was building a competing condominium at the same time and who had filed his offering plan prior to our filing, told our client that he had revised his plan based on ours and that because of the change he had made significantly more money.

In the course of that same development, and in order to facilitate sales, our client wanted to obtain a commitment from a bank to provide mortgage loans to prospective buyers. The cost of the commitment would have been approximately $1,000,000. I argued that anyone who could afford these condominium units would not need a mortgage or would be able to obtain financing without assistance, and, further, that any commitment would have so many contingencies or loopholes that it would be worthless. The client, nevertheless, persisted; but when we obtained a draft of the commitment and I revealed the loopholes, the client relented and agreed to abandon the idea. Financing was never a problem in the sale of any unit. In fact, all sales contracts were signed without a financing contingency—that is, a provision that if the buyer was unable to obtain a loan, the buyer would be released from its obligation to purchase the apartment and the buyer's deposit would be returned.

Too often lawyers, even good, experienced lawyers, will present the various possibilities to the client, perhaps with a weak recommendation, but leave the decision to the client: "It's your money," the lawyer says, tucking the risk of responsibility under his tongue, "so it's your decision to make." On other occasions, a lawyer may allow a forceful client to override the lawyer's judgement, even though the lawyer is convinced the client is making a poor choice: "O.K.," says the lawyer, making the easy choice for herself, "the decision is yours." The choice, of course, is ultimately the client's: The client must decide whose judgement to follow. But the lawyer must not allow the client to make a decision that the lawyer believes is wrong without a forceful and effective presentation by the lawyer of his or her position on the subject. When the matter is within the sphere of the lawyer's expertise, the lawyer must not permit the fear of being wrong to devour the lawyer's obligation to urge a course of action which the lawyer believes to be the best.

§5:4 Proofread Meticulously

Every aspect of writing a contract is essential, even the most menial and boring such as proofreading. Lest there be any doubt, I offer the tragedy of the missing digits reported in an article by David Margolick that appeared in the October 4, 1991 edition of *The New York Times*.

When the financing for a fleet of ships was restructured and the new mortgage prepared, three digits were omitted from a crucial figure. Instead of the mortgage stating that it secured a debt of $92,885,000, it stated that it secured a debt of $92,885—not an insubstantial difference. Although this error appeared in almost 100 documents, none of the law firms that worked on the transaction, not even the mortgagee's in-house counsel, detected the error. After the litigation cleared, the mortgagee "reckoned that the typo had cost it at least $31 million".

But there is another aspect of Mr. Margolick's article that deserves attention. The article reports that the firm responsible for preparing the mortgage "knew the name of the erring secretary", whom the firm described as contrite and of unknown whereabouts. The implication that the secretary was to blame is outrageous. Secretaries type thousands upon thousands of characters an hour. No one knows how many errors will occur or how serious they will be; but everyone knows they will occur. The person ultimately responsible for accuracy is the lawyer, not the secretary. By the time the document is presented for signature, "typos" do not exist; they have been superseded by proofreading errors and by "lawyeros". The lawyer must assume this responsibility—not drown it in the typing pool.

§5:5 Respond Appropriately to the Other Party's Draft

There are four primary ways to respond initially to the draft of an agreement: by telephone; by a meeting; by preparing a new draft; by noting changes on the original draft.

If there are only a few points that do not involve major issues or revisions, then response by telephone may be the most efficient way to reply. The lawyers can discuss the points and agree to any changes. To expedite the discussion, the person responding to the draft should prepare, before making the call, any suggested changes in wording.

A meeting is only necessary if there are major issues to discuss, but I cannot recall a situation in which I responded initially by a meeting. I would first give the other party written comments to clearly delineate the issues. This initial response provides the foundation and agenda for discussion; it allows the other party to study, without the pressure of an immediate reply, your client's concerns and, perhaps, to develop alternate suggestions to accommodate those concerns; it reduces the risk of proposals being made that have to be changed or withdrawn later because they were formulated quickly without adequate consideration. In essence, producing written comments first results in a more efficient and effective meeting.

I try at all costs to avoid rewriting the agreement and presenting the other side with a new draft—even a draft marked to show changes. I doubt that anything infuriates a lawyer more than expending the time and effort to prepare a document only to receive a totally new document in reply. Even if the changes from the original draft are marked, the attorney *must*, nevertheless, compare the new draft against the original to be sure the changes are correctly identified. Also, while it is relatively easy to focus on additions, the lawyer must return to his or her original draft to understand deletions. In effect, the lawyer must now work with two documents. Thus, I only prepare a new draft—and it is rare that I do—if the original document is written so poorly that it defies comprehension or if the original document is virtually unresponsive to the needs of our client (as to this latter point, see Chapter 4).

The way I usually respond, and the way I prefer to respond, is to mark deletions on the original draft and to add text by riders and handwritten inserts to that draft. The appendix to this chapter contains an example. This procedure gives the other side, in a single document, a comprehensive view of the issues and proposed solutions. It focuses and, therefore, facilitates discussion. Often the attorneys can resolve all or most of the problems by telephone, thereby narrowing the scope (and thus the cost) of any meeting that might be required. In most contractual matters, I find marking the changes on the initial draft the most effective, efficient response.

§5:6 Be Efficient in Preparing the Documentation

This word "efficient" is appearing quite often. It must be important.

It is. Unfortunately, lawyers who charge by the hour make money by inefficiency. But clients, ever more wary of legal costs, are becoming more demanding. Recently, our firm gained two new clients on recommendations because their former attorneys were inefficient and unresponsive.

Perhaps there are good lawyers, even great lawyers, who are not very efficient. But, as a general rule, to be a good lawyer, the lawyer must be efficient. And in the realm of commercial transactions, efficiency means organizing and ordering the various components of the transaction and vigorously pursuing them to conclusion. It helps to be compulsive; luckily most attorneys are.

Also luckily (though I know the publisher will fret about the length of this book—or lack thereof), I need not attempt to solve the reader's insomnia with a treatise on efficiency. The key tool is located in Chapter 3: the outline (not the term sheet, because the term sheet may omit certain legal and business considerations which the outline will contain). The lawyer need only hitch his or her compulsion to that instrument and engage the warp drive.

In the realm that joins theory and practicality, efficiency mightily serves the prime directive. No trickster induces error with greater frequency than pressure, requiring tasks to be performed more quickly than they should be. Efficiency diffuses that pressure, creating the mental space required to allow the mind to perform comfortably. The result is fewer errors.

Just two more points: *first*, return phone calls promptly; *second*, don't wait until the last minute to attend to details that seem of minor importance, such as preparing and adopting the corporate resolutions. In fact, one of the first items on the agenda that I complete is the corporate action to eliminate that detail.

§5:7 Understand the Difference between the Active and Passive Voices; Know When to Use the Passive Voice

In the active voice, the subject of the verb performs the action:

John ate the frog.

In the passive voice, the subject of the verb is the object of the action:

The *frog* was eaten by John.

Thus, as a general rule, the passive voice should be used when the result of the action is the essence of the message and the doer of the action is either unimportant or unknown or the person making the statement wishes to be vague:

The rain forests are being destroyed. We will perish.

Use the active voice when the action and the doer of the action are the important parts of the message:

Pollution and urbanization are destroying the rain forests. We will perish.

Stylists prefer the active voice because the statements generally are shorter and more direct and, therefore, more forceful than statements in the passive voice:

> I shall cherish the gift always.

> *vs.*

> This gift will be cherished by me always.

However, in the contract, where loopholes are the enemy and the force of the statement is irrelevant, the passive voice is sometimes the shorter and safer route to comprehensiveness. For example:

> If you damage the equipment, you will repair it.

But someone else might damage the equipment. Therefore:

> If you or anyone else damages the equipment,...

Still, lightning or falling rocks or an avalanche might damage the equipment. Thus:

> If you or anyone else or anything damages the equipment,...

Yet, what if the equipment is parked on a hill and the brake slips, and the equipment rolls down the hill into a mud pond fouling all of its parts? The last version should cover the situation, but I would not want to argue the point. So:

> If you or anyone else or anything damages the equipment or the equipment becomes damaged in any other manner,...

Or, more simply, use the passive voice when the result of the action is the essence of the message and how it occurs is immaterial:

> If the equipment is damaged,...

Another example? The passive voice is sometimes the better choice in default clauses:

> If a petition is filed by or against you in a bankruptcy or other insolvency proceeding and, if against you, it is not dismissed within thirty days, ...

vs.

> If you file a petition in a bankruptcy or other insolvency proceeding or if anyone files a petition against you in any such proceeding and the court does not dismiss it within thirty days, ...

Sometimes the conjunction "if" or the verb "becomes" are signals to consider the passive voice. But the draftsman must beware of the passive voice when the doer of the action is essential to the intended result. Thus, note the difference:

> If the house is sold, I will pay you ...

vs.

> If you sell the house, I will pay you ...

Perhaps in the contract, where the force of the statement is not important, the passive voice has greater use than in other forms of writing; but the draftsman must not take this thought as an endorsement for the wanton use of the passive voice:

> Passivable: The following services will be performed by you for which you will be paid by the company $_____ per day ...

> Preferable: You will perform the following services for which the company will pay you $_____ per day ...

(Note: Despite the last example, this section has been sponsored by the Passive Voice Anti-Defamation League.)

§5:8 Additional Tools

As a writer, the commercial lawyer should have two reference works to help implement the first half of the prime directive: a dictionary and a grammar book. The one-volume dictionary which I use (under mandate from my wife, the English teacher) and which I recommend is *Webster's New World Dictionary, Third College Edition.* (The only time I use a law dictionary is to answer questions of my secretary about Latin phrases she comes across when typing briefs to help out the litigation department.)

The grammar book which I use (also under mandate from the Boss) and which I recommend is the *Harbrace College Handbook.*

There is a third book, which normally modesty would enjoin me from suggesting; but, with Thornton Wilder as a precedent (*Our Town,* Stage Manager, Act One), I will just mention it: *Commercial Agreements: A Lawyer's Guide to Drafting and Negotiating, supra.*

Appendix to Chapter 5

3. *(a)* In consideration of the covenants and undertakings set forth herein, Employee hereby covenants not to sue and hereby voluntarily releases and forever discharges the Corporation from liability for any and all acts or omissions of the Corporation, including, but not limited to,...

— RIDER 3 (b) see following page

neither the Employee nor

5. This Agreement has been entered into solely to avoid the burdens and expense of litigation. By entering into this Agreement and its terms, the Corporation ~~does not~~ admit*s* to any acts of wrongdoing or any liability to ~~Employee~~ *the other* or to any other person or entity.

and the Corporation each

7. Employee agrees that he *or it, as the case may be,* will not at any time (a) publicly disparage or encourage or induce others to publicly disparage the ~~Corporation;~~ *other;* and/or, (b) engage in any conduct that is in any way injurious to the reputation and interests of the ~~Cor-poration~~ *other* (including, without limitation, any negative or derogatory statements or writings).

RIDER 3(b)

(b) In consideration of the covenants and undertakings set forth herein, the Corporation hereby covenants not to sue and hereby voluntarily releases and forever discharges Employee from liability for any and all acts or omissions of Employee, including, but not limited to,...

Chapter 6

Amending Contracts; Using Forms[*]

Amending a contract, at least for me, is more difficult than writing the initial agreement because, frequently, changing but one term may require compensating or conforming changes to other provisions. The addition of a new section to a contract illustrates the point. The new section will require renumbering of the sections that follow. In addition, the lawyer must check the entire contract for references to those renumbered sections; and still further, the lawyer must examine the contract—*as well as any companion or related contracts*—to determine whether other provisions require change by reason of the addition. To a certain extent, the computer will help. For example, a defined term must be deleted from a contract. The computer program will locate all uses of the defined term in order to delete them; but the lawyer must also review the entire agreement to determine how to amend those sentences in which the defined term is used and to see whether other changes are needed because of the deletion. Amending a contract is a demanding exercise that the lawyer must execute diligently in order to avoid error.

———————

[*] This chapter is based on Siviglia, *Commercial Agreements, supra,* §1:4.

The method of amending a contract also requires special care. Sometimes lawyers will amend a contract in the following manner:

> The agreement dated _____, 199_ between ___A___ and ___B___ is amended to provide that ___B___ will....

This format should not be used because a general statement such as this may result in ambiguity and dispute: Its effect on the specific terms of the agreement may be unclear. Thus, each provision affected by the change must be located and amended appropriately. The process amounts to a surgical procedure. The amendment should (1) revise the text of each provision to be changed, (2) state the effective date of the amendment and, if relevant, whether the version of the agreement prior to its amendment will continue to govern any particular matters, and (3) confirm that the contract as amended remains in effect. For example:

> The agreement dated _____, 199_ between ___A___ and ___B___ is amended, effective _____, 199_, as follows.

1. The figure "$___X___" in Section 3 of the agreement is deleted wherever it appears in that Section, and the figure "$___Y___" is substituted in its place.

2. The second sentence of Section 4 of the agreement is amended in its entirety to read as follows:

   _____

   _____

   _____

   _____.

3. Following Section 5 of the agreement, a new Section 6 is added as follows:

6.   _____
     _____
     _____
     _____.

4.   Sections 6, 7, 8 and 9 of the agreement are
renumbered 7, 8, 9 and 10 respectively.

As hereinabove amended, the agreement will remain in
full force and effect [; but the agreement as it existed
prior to the effective date of this amendment will govern
those matters listed on Exhibit A hereto].

Many lawyers write the last sentence: "Except as hereinabove amended, the contract will remain in full force and
effect." I do not know why they use the word "except", and I
have never received a satisfactory explanation for its use. The
word seems to cancel the amendment or to place it in some
amorphous state. Thus "as", rather than "except", is the
word to use.

Long ago and far away in Chapter 1, I noted that forms
are useful and necessary tools. A caution, though, is worth
mention: The same principles and discipline required to
amend a contract must be applied to the use of a form. Like
snowflakes, no two transactions are the same. Thus, no matter how basic a provision may seem, the lawyer must examine
it carefully to determine whether changes are required to con-
form it to the particular transaction. The danger in using a
form is adopting the text without critical examination. Forms
prompt laziness and dull the defenses. The lawyer must be
alert to these dangers and aware that a form will not fit a
transaction just by completing blanks or substituting alternate
clauses. If the form fits precisely, the fit is purely by coinci-
dence. Writing a contract cannot be reduced to a practice by
the numbers. If it could, little need would remain for the commercial lawyer.

Chapter 7

The Quest for Simplicity

§7:1 Introduction

As observed in Chapter 2, at least in the realm of writing contracts, the degree of simplicity that the draftsman can achieve is often a function of the concepts with which the draftsman must work—the first duty of the draftsman being to convey the message correctly.

Nevertheless, I hate complexity. Not only are complex concepts difficult to write, but the writing is difficult to read and to understand. I have seen transactions fail because they were just too complex and too difficult to execute. From the draftsman's point of view, complexity intensifies the risk of error in the drafting and the risk of different interpretations in the reading: both chum for the litigators. The commercial attorney, therefore, must work to achieve a result as simple as possible. And to accomplish this goal, the attorney must exorcise two demons: sloth and the fear of being original.

§7:2 Structure

Lawyers confront the challenge to simplify on two levels: structural and textual. To face the structural challenge the lawyer must pry open the transaction and examine its contents with the view to developing, in the least complicated manner, an effective response to the requirements of the deal. Often, a simple solution is the best solution. For example,...

Remember the inventor in §5:2 of Chapter 5 who was seeking to acquire certain patent applications from his former employer? The initial conception of the transaction by the inventor and his attorneys before asking our firm to assist was *first*, to sign a contract with the former employer providing for transfer of the patent applications to him within six months after the date of signing; *second*, with transfer of the applications secured by that contract, to raise funds from outside inventors to provide working capital to perfect and exploit the patents; and *then* to complete the transfer of the applications under the contract and begin the new business.

When we explored the transaction with our new client, we learned that he had no experience in running a business and, consequently, would need the assistance of an executive officer to manage the company. In addition, to complete the transaction in accordance with the original plan (1) the services of an investment banker would have to be engaged to raise the venture capital; (2) because our client lacked the ability to operate the business, the executive officer would also have to be hired to attract this investment; (3) in addition, potential investors would have to be offered a substantial equity position in the new company; (4) our client would have to commit his services to the new company for a significant period and would have to agree to non-compete restrictions both during and after his employment; and (5) if the venture failed, there would be a substantial risk that the investors, who had lost their money, would bring a lawsuit against the client asserting the usual allegations including failure to disclose material information and fraud. Further, the cost of these arrangements would be substantial without any certainty (A) that they could be made, and (B) even if they could be made, that they could be concluded within the contemplated six-month period. What was certain, though, was that the former employer would not enter into a deal contingent on our client's making these arrangements.

Thus, from our discussions, it quickly became apparent that the original concept was impractical and unworkable. The design was inappropriate and too involved. Pursuing it would have been a disaster for the client. However, the discussions did reveal that our client could easily exploit the applications and achieve a better and less costly result (1) by licensing the applications and the resulting patents, and (2) if he and the licensee so agreed, by contracting with the licensee to assist the licensee in perfecting and developing the patents and the underlying products. We, therefore, abandoned the venture capital scheme with all of its complications and adopted the simpler approach: transferring the patent applications to our client immediately on signing the contract with his former employer. While we negotiated the contracts, our client explored potential licensing arrangements.

To design the best framework for the transaction, an inquisitive and flexible approach is essential when vetting the transaction with the client.

§7:3 Text

The second level of confrontation occurs in the documents themselves. There is a story, perhaps apocryphal, that depicts the combat zone. A senior partner in a venerable law firm asked a young associate to adapt one of the firm's trust indentures to a new transaction. A trust indenture is a long, complicated document used in financing transactions. The associate went to work and after a few days presented the partner with a much simpler version of the indenture. After reviewing the draft, the partner asked the young attorney into his office and commented: "This is a wonderful job. It's much more simple; it's well written; and it's understandable—but we can't use it. Practically every sentence in our form is based on a court decision dealing with that language. We dare not change the form."

The partner's decision was not wrong. It was prudently cautious. But the young associate also was not wrong. What he did was adventurous and well executed, even though he probably did not realize the adventure he was taking.

Certainly lawyers must not practice their profession in a way that risks their clients' money, but I do not consider simplification a risk. In fact, I consider "simple" safe, even when "simple" requires a departure from the traditional. A perfect example is the Coastal States' guarantee discussed in §1:3 of Chapter 1. When I wrote that guarantee, I did not consider it either adventurous or risky. But the partners did. "Where did you get that form?", they asked after the default had occurred. When I told them I had invented it, they became concerned; but their nerves were relieved by the judge's decision.

——————

As stated in Chapter 2 and reiterated above, sometimes an involved concept will, of necessity, produce complexity in the writing. However, the formula that follows breaches the barrier separating the rational from the insane. The purpose of the formula is to determine the amount of the premium which the borrower must pay the lender on prepayment of the loan. The premium is based on the difference between the interest rate on the loan and the prevailing interest rate at the time of prepayment. The formula actually comprised part of the loan documentation of a major New York bank. Mercifully, I omitted an entire page of definitions, which are not needed to make the point.

Mathematical Formula

If the Borrower elects a fixed interest rate, then the Borrower may prepay the Note in whole, but not in part, on not less than three (3) business days prior written notice to the Lender accompanied by payment of a premium, if any, equal to the sum of the present values, each determined at the appropriate Discount Rate, of the excess, if any, of (A) the amount of interest computed at Lender's Cost Rate on the principal amount of the Note (after giving effect to any scheduled amortization occurring prior to the first day of each Determination Period) deemed to be due on the last day of each Determination Period during the remaining term of the Note, over (B) the amount of each corresponding interest payment computed at the Reinvestment Rate. Such present value shall be computed according to the following formula:

$$PV = \sum_{n=1}^{n=DP} NET_n$$

$$NET_n = \cfrac{(P \times [LCR - RR]) \times \cfrac{Days_n - Days_{n-1}}{360}}{\cfrac{Days_n - Days_0}{360}}$$

$$(1 + Q_n) \; [sic]$$

$Days_n$ - $Days_{n-1}$ = For each Determination Period "n", the actual number of days elapsed during that Determination Period.

$Days_n$ - $Days_0$ = For each Determination Period "n", the actual number of days elapsed from the date of prepayment to the last day of that Determination Period.

DP = Number, or fraction thereof, of Determination Periods from date of prepayment to date of final fixed maturity of the Note.

LCR = Lender's Cost Rate

P = Principal amount being prepaid

Q = For each Determination Period "n", the Discount Rate for that Determination Period.

RR = Reinvestment Rate

I originally planned to cage this monster in an appendix, but it depicts so sharply what the lawyer must never do that I could not tuck the impact away in a caboose. Without a doubt, it violates one of the Chapter 2 rules: "Do not include in a contract a provision which you do not understand." If a dispute arose, both sides would call mathematicians as expert witnesses to explain the formula; and, of course, the only winners would be the litigators.

The lawyer must battle to express accurately and understandably difficult concepts. Even the equation quoted above can be stated in English, and, with the reader's indulgence, following is an adaptation. The definition of "Reinvestment Rate" is not required for the illustration, so I have omitted it. Though the translation to English is complex, one does not have to be a mathematician to understand it. The translation is based on a discount clause that I had previously used. Following the directions of that clause, both the lender and the borrower calculated the amount of the discount identically.

If the maker of the note elects the note to bear a fixed interest rate [as opposed to a floating rate that changes with changes in the interest rate market], then for as long as the interest rate under the note is a fixed rate, the maker may, upon not less than three (3) business days prior written notice to the payee, prepay the outstanding principal in whole only and not in part, together with (i) accrued interest thereon to and including the date of prepayment, and (ii) the prepayment premium, if any, as hereinafter determined. Such notice must specify the date on which the prepayment is to be made by the maker.

If the fixed rate of interest under the note exceeds the "Reinvestment Rate" [definition omitted], then, concurrently with the prepayment, the maker will pay to the payee a prepayment premium equal to *the sum of the present values* (each *present value* to be determined with respect to each three-month interest period under the note) *of the difference between*

(A) the amount of interest for the interest period in question computed at the note's fixed rate applied to the principal balance of the note on the first day of such interest period on the assumption that all installments of principal payable on or prior to the first day of such interest period will have been paid, and

(B) the amount of interest for the interest period in question computed at the Reinvestment Rate applied to the principal balance of the note as determined under (A) above.

The *present value* of each *difference* for each interest period will be that amount which when added to interest thereon at the Reinvestment Rate compounded every three (3) months from the date of the prepayment to and including the last day of the applicable interest period will equal the amount of that *difference.*

The lawyer must not assume that a statement—because it was written by a senior person, because it has the authority of being part of an institution's standard documentation, because it was written by the very lawyer—is the best statement of the message. The lawyer, in the mandatory procedures of reviewing and editing the document, must examine each passage critically for accuracy and ease of statement.

Less dramatic than the equation, yet an effective illustration of editorial anemia, is the following passage, which, like the meanderings of a drunken duck, confounds the reader, barely passing the "accuratalyzer" test:

> The Company will retain exclusive worldwide marketing rights with respect to any products and uses thereof developed by Dr. Lovejoy, his agents and assignees in the ___ABC___ fields which use confidential information disclosed to Dr. Lovejoy during, or known by Dr. Lovejoy as a result of, his employment by the Company, including specifically, but not limited to, information derived by Dr. Lovejoy in whole or in part from research engaged in by him or others during the term of his employment by the Company, not generally known in the trade or industry in which the Company is engaged, about the Company's products, processes, machines, and services, including research (specifically, but not limited to, Dr. Lovejoy's research while employed by the Company), development, manufacturing, purchasing, finance, data processing, engineering, marketing, merchandising and selling.

It is truly remarkable that well-educated adults earn substantial sums of money to produce these insults to the reader, when, with a bit of effort, they could easily have sobered the poor little bird:

> The Company will retain exclusive worldwide marketing rights with respect to any products and uses thereof developed by Dr. Lovejoy, his agents and assignees in the ___ABC___ fields which use confidential information about products, processes, machines and services of the Company (including research, development, manufacturing, purchasing, finance, data processing, engineering, marketing, merchandising and selling) (A) that is disclosed to Dr. Lovejoy during or known by Dr. Lovejoy as a result of his employment by the Company, and (B) that is not generally known in the trade or industry in which the Company is engaged. Confidential information includes, but is not limited to, information derived by Dr. Lovejoy in whole or in part from research in which he or others engaged during the term of his employment by the Company and that is not generally known in the trade or industry in which the Company is engaged.

As observed at the opening of the chapter, laziness and fear are the roots of complexity. These traits often flower in the form of overwriting. Several times I have seen a demand promissory note containing default clauses. When I ask the purpose of these default clauses, since the note *is* payable on demand, the author replies: "They make me feel more comfortable." If I were representing the lender, though, their presence would make me nervous because they violate yet another of the Chapter 2 rules: "Do not include a provision that undermines another provision." For example, if the lender demands payment when a default does not exist, the borrower, if it wanted to delay, might argue that the demand was made in bad faith and so should not be honored. This argument should lose, but the document, in the first place, should not provide fuel for the argument. On the other hand, if the lender demands payment asserting a default, the borrower may challenge the default and argue that the demand is improper. In either case, the result is the same: the availability of an argument that should not exist.

Examples of overwriting abound, but one more will serve the point. An employer agreed to make a severance payment to its departing employee of $500,000. This amount was payable in periodic installments until the occurrence of one of three events. On the occurrence of that event, the employer agreed to pay the employee the remaining balance of the $500,000 regardless of whether the employee had breached the terms of the severance agreement. Omitting irrelevant language, the severance agreement prepared by the employer accomplished this result as follows:

3. Your termination date...will be the earliest to occur of August 17, 1995 or the date on which you become actively employed with another firm or the date the Firm terminates your payroll status as provided in Paragraph 4b below [default].

4. You will receive a separation payment in the amount of $500,000...according to the following schedule:

   a. Subject to Paragraph 4b below [default], you will be paid on a biweekly basis at your current biweekly base salary rate of $_____ from February 20, 1995, through either August 17, 1995, or the date on which you become actively employed with another Firm, whichever comes first, while you remain on payroll and continue your benefits coverage under the terms of our plans.... You will then receive a lump sum payment representing the remainder of the $500,000 within three weeks of August 17, 1995 or three weeks after we are notified of your employment with another firm....

   b. If...you have breached the terms of this Agreement, the Firm may terminate your payroll status at that time. If your payroll status is terminated,

you will then receive a lump sum payment representing the remainder of the $500,000 within three
weeks after your termination date.

Yet all of the verbiage in paragraphs 4a and 4b could have
been reduced to the following:

a.   We will pay you $_____ biweekly until your ter-
     mination date. We will then pay you the remainder
     of the $500,000 within three weeks after your ter-
     mination date; or, if you become employed by
     another firm, within three weeks after you notify
     us of that employment....
b.   If...you breach this Agreement, the Firm may ter-
     minate your employment status.

The result is the same under both versions, but the second
version is shorter, easier to understand and directly to the
point. The first is more involved, and it is also confusing
because it defines "your termination date" and then ignores
that definition in paragraph 4a. I suggested the simpler version to the attorney for the employer, but the attorney reject-
ed the suggestion, offering the customary reply: "Cosi fan
tutti" [That's the way we do it].

§7:4   Coda

"'Tis the gift to be simple", proclaims the nineteenth century Shaker hymn, "Simple Gifts". From the foregoing examples, though, it is apparent that some lawyers do not receive
this gift; or if they do receive it, they lose it somewhere in law
school and the hunt for partnership. But the "gift" can be
acquired; it can be learned; yet, despite the rules and techniques discussed in Chapter 2, I doubt that the "gift" can be
taught. Thus, making the reader sensitive to the need to simplify and aware of the value of simplification is the most that
I can hope this chapter will accomplish. The lawyer must inte-

grate this conviction into his or her "lawyerness" and expend the effort to achieve the result.

On the structural level, the ability to simplify requires common sense and experience, which the alert lawyer will develop in the course of his or her practice.

On the textual level, an awareness and an understanding of the language are essential. These are qualities that the student should have acquired, at least to some extent, before entering law school; but they are qualities that certainly can and must be developed and improved thereafter. These qualities, when combined with the patience and commitment to examine the text critically, will produce a good contract.

Chapter 8

Commencement

Be alert to the transaction....
Be alert to the text....
Go forth and contract.

About the Author

Peter Siviglia received a B.A. from Williams College in 1961, an M.A. from Brown University in 1962, and a J.D. from Harvard University in 1965. Since graduating from law school, he has practiced law in New York, representing entrepreneurs, banks and corporations in transactions, both domestic and international, involving coprorate matters, finance, intellectual property, real estate, acquisitions and shipping. His publications include *Exercises in Commercial Transactions* (Carolina Academic Press), *Commercial Agreements: A Lawyer's Guide to Drafting and Negotiating* (West Group), and numerous articles on writing contracts and other legal topics.